Racecars
Go Fast

KINGFISHER
NEW YORK

KINGFISHER
LONDON & NEW YORK

Copyright © Kingfisher 2012
Published in the United States by Kingfisher,
175 Fifth Ave., New York, NY 10010
Kingfisher is an imprint of Macmillan Children's Books, London.

Written and designed by Dynamo Ltd.

Distributed in the U.S. and Canada by Macmillan,
175 Fifth Ave., New York, NY 10010

Library of Congress Cataloging-in-Publication data has been applied for.

ISBN 978-0-7534-7008-4

Kingfisher books are available for special promotions and premiums. For details contact:
Special Markets Department, Macmillan, 175 Fifth Ave., New York, NY 10010.

For more information, please visit www.kingfisherbooks.com

Printed in China
9 8 7 6 5 4 3 2 1
1TR/0612/HH/-/140MA

Contents

4 Why do planes have wings?

6 Which planes go the fastest?

8 How can bicycles ride down mountains?

10 Why do trains have metal wheels?

12 Why do racecars go so fast?

14 How do boats float?

16 What did old sailing ships look like?

18 Why do trucks have big wheels?

20 Which trucks are the longest in the world?

22 What do you know about machines that go?

24 Some machine words

Why do planes have wings?

As a plane flies along, air flows around its wings. The wings are curved on top and flat underneath.

Air flows faster across the top of the wings than it does underneath them. The fast-flowing air sucks the wings upward, keeping the plane in the sky.

All about airplanes

- Passenger planes carry many people.
- They fly high above the clouds.
- They travel very fast, sometimes over 500 miles (800 kilometers) per hour.

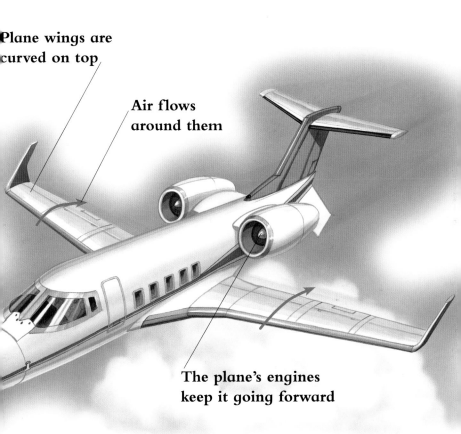

Plane wings are
curved on top

Air flows
around them

The plane's engines
keep it going forward

5

Which planes go the fastest?

The fastest aircraft are planes with powerful jet engines. The jet engines burn fuel to make gases called exhaust.

The exhaust gases shoot out of the back of the plane, helping push it forward.

All about jet planes

- Jets can fly higher than other aircraft, as well as faster.
- The latest jet designs are for unmanned jets, with no pilot onboard.
- The fastest ever jet plane, called Blackbird, once flew at 2,193 miles (3,530km) per hour.

Many jet planes are
shaped like an arrow

The arrow shape helps
the plane speed through
the air

How can bicycles ride down mountains?

Mountain bikes can go over rough, stony ground.

The frame of a mountain bike is extrastrong, and its thick, knobby tires are good for riding over lumps and bumps.

All about bicycles

- Racing bikes look different to mountain bikes. They have thin tires and light frames to help them go fast.
- The first bicycles ever invented had no pedals. Riders pushed them along with their feet.
- Tandem bicycles have seats for two riders—one behind the other.

A mountain bike can cope with a lot of rattling and bumping

The tires are good at gripping onto bumpy ground

9

Why do trains have metal wheels?

A train runs along narrow metal rails.

The train wheels fit over the rails and keep the train in place.

All about trains

- The fastest trains in the world can travel more than 250 miles (400km) in an hour.

- Passenger trains carry people around the country.

- Freight (fr-ay-t) trains carry goods, not passengers.

A train can only
travel on top of
a railway line

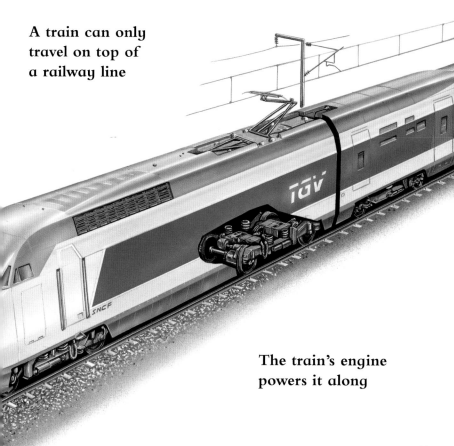

The train's engine
powers it along

11

Why do racecars go so fast?

Racecars have very powerful engines. Power from the engine turns the wheels.

Racecars are shaped so that they cut through the air smoothly as they race forward.

All about racecars

- There are many different kinds of racecars.
- Racecars make more noise than ordinary cars because their engines are more powerful.
- The world's fastest car set a speed record of over 760 miles (1,228km) per hour.

A dragster is a superfast racecar shaped like a long, thin arrow

The dragster goes so fast it needs a parachute to help it slow down

13

How do boats float?

A boat stays afloat because when it pushes down on water, the water pushes back up on the boat.

Boats are shaped so that they are not too heavy to float, and they won't easily roll over.

Boats big and small

- The biggest ships in the world are supertankers, which carry oil.

- Supertankers can be more than one third of a mile (0.5km) long.

- Yachts can go very fast through the water. They sometimes race one another.

A yacht has
sails to help it
move along

The sails catch the
wind, pushing the
yacht forward

15

What did old sailing ships look like?

In the past, all ships were made of wood. They did not have engines, only sails to push them along.

The sails were fixed to long wooden poles called masts.

All about sailing ships

- Big sailing ships had three masts and lots of differently shaped sails.
- The sails were controlled by ropes called rigging.
- To go faster, the crew would put up more sails.

Wind pushed against
the sails and moved
the ship along

Sailors worked
hard to pull
the sails up
or down

17

Why do trucks have big wheels?

Trucks need big wheels because they are very heavy. The wheels must be strong and thick to hold up a truck.

Truck tires have zigzag patterns on them, called tread. The tread helps them grip onto the ground.

All about trucks

- There are many different kinds of trucks for doing different jobs.
- Dump trucks can carry a heavy load. They tip up to pour out the load.
- The biggest dump trucks carry rock and earth from mines and quarries.

Dump trucks have the
biggest wheels—some are
more than 11 ft. (3.6m) high

19

Which are the longest trucks in the world?

The longest trucks are called longer combination vehicles (LCVs) or "triples." They pull more than one trailer at once.

LCVs are useful for driving across empty areas of country where there are no railways.

All about LCVs

- The biggest LCVs are used in Australia.
- The longest ever LCV pulled 112 trailers.
- Some LCVs have only three or four long trucks.

The truck at the front of an LCV has a big, powerful engine

The truck must be strong to pull the heavily loaded trailers

What do you know about machines that go?

You can find all of the answers to these questions in this book.

If you were going to ride along a rough, stony path, would you use a mountain bike or a racing bike?

Why are jet planes shaped like arrows?

What does a freight train carry? Is it goods or passengers?

22

Is a dragster a type of car or a type of airplane?

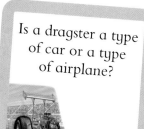

Do you know what the longest trucks in the world are called?

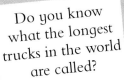

What does a supertanker carry? Is it oil or people?

Some machine words

Engine The part of a machine that burns fuel to make power.

Exhaust Gases that are made when an engine burns fuel.

Freight Goods that a train, a truck, or a ship might carry.

Passenger Someone who rides in a machine such as a train or a ship.

Rail A long strip of metal laid across the ground, for trains to run along.

Rigging The ropes on a sailing ship.

Tread The zigzag pattern on a tire.